F THIS TEST

F THIS TEST

Even More of the Very Best Totally Wrong Test Answers

Richard Benson

CHRONICLE BOOKS

SAN FRANCISCO

First published in the United States in 2014 by Chronicle Books LLC.

The contents of this book were published in the United Kingdom in 2012 by Summersdale
Publishers Ltd. under the titles *F in English*, *F in Geography*, *F in History*, *F in Retakes*, and
F in Science. Copyright © 2012 by Summersdale Publishers Ltd. All rights reserved. No
part of this book may be reproduced in any form without permission from the publisher.

Library of Congress Cataloging-in-Publication Data

Benson, Richard.
  F this test : even more of the very best totally wrong test answers / Richard Benson.
    pages cm
ISBN 978-1-4521-2776-7 (pbk.)
1. Education—Humor. 2. Examinations—Humor. I. Title.
LB3051.B397 2014
370.2—dc23

                        2013032178

Manufactured in China

MIX
Paper from
responsible sources
FSC® C008047

Designed by Liam Flanagan

10 9 8 7 6

Chronicle Books LLC
680 Second Street
San Francisco, California 94107
www.chroniclebooks.com

Contents

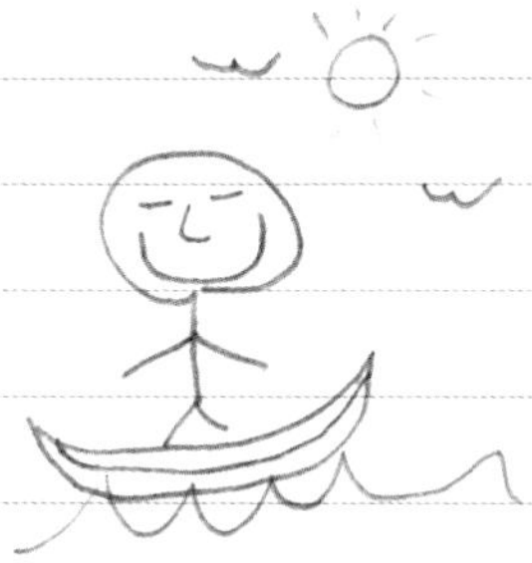

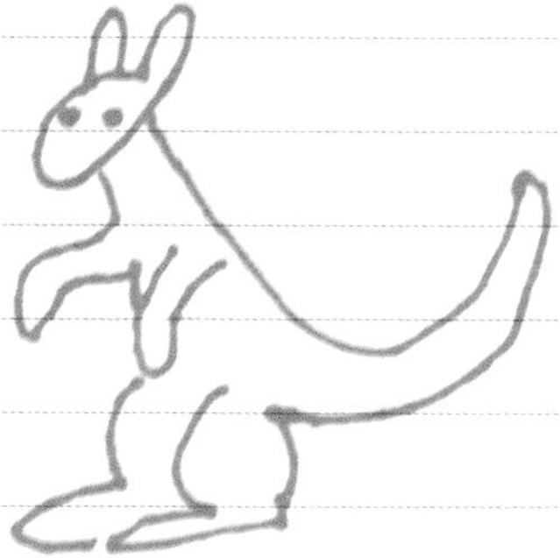

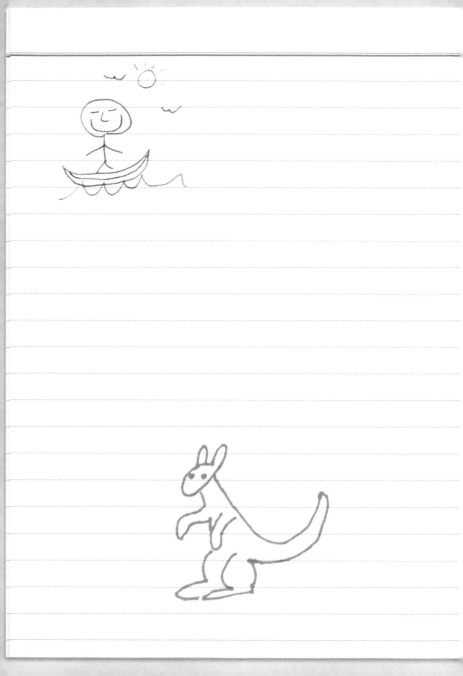

Introduction

School can be fun. If you know all the answers, filling out a test paper can be

a) A snap

b) A breeze

c) A cinch

d) All of the above

But of course there are those times when you don't know the answers. We've all been there: You look at the question, read it again, skip it, come back to it later, and still draw a total blank.

Faced with this catastrophe, the students whose real test answers are collected here didn't give up. They decided to have a little fun instead, and their answers—wrong, but brilliantly wrong—should earn them extra credit, if school or life was remotely fair.

While, alas, their grades may have suffered, their collected efforts are here at least for us to enjoy.

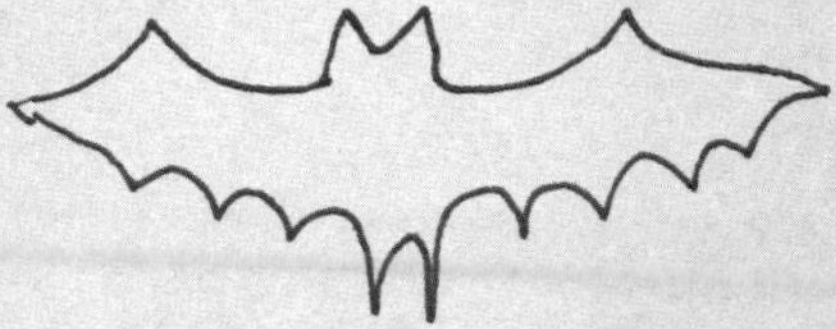

Subject: English

How does Dickens create sympathy for Pip in *Great Expectations*?

He gives him a girl's name

List the main events of *Robinson Crusoe*.

Robinson goes on a cruise.

What is the overall message of *Frankenstein*?

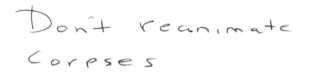

Name a key theme in *Madame Bovary*.

Summarize the events of *The Fall of the House of Usher*.

Building mishaps occur.

Give a brief summary of the plot of *The Strange Case of Dr. Jekyll and Mr. Hyde*.

Jekyll & Hyde find a briefcase, and it's very strange.

List two major themes of *The Strange Case of Dr. Jekyll and Mr. Hyde*.

Dr. Jekyll   Mr. Hyde.

How is Piggy made sympathetic in *The Lord of the Flies*?

His little curly tail.

How are the mountain range's conditions described in *Touching the Void*?

The mountains are portrayed as being high and pointy, with some snowy parts and some not so

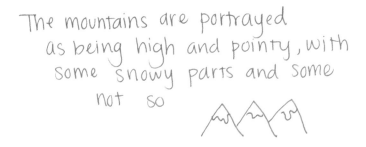

What factors lead toward Nancy's death in *Oliver Twist*?

CHARLES DICKENS KILLED HER.

How might the themes of *Crime and Punishment* be relevant to today's society?

It's been adapted into a TV show called Law and Order.

List two ways *Pride and Prejudice* can be read.

1. Sitting down, book on lap.
2. Lying down.

Name three tenses.

STRESSED, WORRIED, AND CONCERNED.

Give an example of a proverb.

A JOURNEY of a thousand miles is as good as a rest to a blind horse that gathers no moss for want of a shoe.

Give an example of a sentence containing a suffix.

SUFFIX IT TO SAY,
I WON'T BE GOING
BACK THERE AGAIN.

Write a sentence containing a double negative.

Mike is ugly and he smells.

mike →

In what sort of writing would it be appropriate to use bullet points?

In what circumstances would you employ a semicolon?

When they have a good
C.V. and interview

When would you use a preposition?.

When you want to marry someone.

Which sentence is correct?

Please tell Damien if there are less than five books in the library.

Please tell Damien if there are fewer than five books in the library.

Neither, libraries should always have more than five books.

On average, how many words a minute do we usually speak?

IT VARIES, DEPENDING ON HOW ANNOYING YOU ARE.

How significant is tone of voice when communicating?

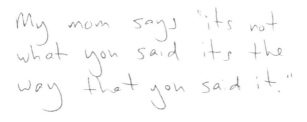

My mom says "its not what you said its the way that you said it."

Write a sentence containing a "question tag."

I should know what
it is, shouldn't I?

Define dialect.

Dr. Whos biggest enemies
were the dialects

When people from a particular area share a way of speaking it is called:

Inside Jokes

What is a sonnet?

What a mommet and a poppet give birth to

When writing to argue, what techniques might you use to gain the readers' attention?

Writing in
CAPITAL LETTERS.

Give two techniques writers use to create atmosphere

. A few drinks
. Some good friends

Give the correct opening for writing a formal letter to a person you don't know.

Opening: "Who are you?"

Why should an author keep their audience in mind?

Because if they kept them in real life that would be Kidnapping

What sort of terms are "you have to," "you must," and "you ought to"?

The sort my mom uses too often.

What is the effect of imperatives?

They make you poo

Using the works you have studied, give an example of a heroic couplet.

BATMAN AND ROBIN

Give an example of a "purpose."

They've quite like dolphins.

Define "embody."

The thing beneath
Em's head.

Emhead

Embody

What is melodrama?

It's the opposite of
angry drama

Name a key plot device in a comedy of manners.

A person who does
not say "please"
and "Thank you!"

Define "ambiguity."

The point of ambiguity
is that it can't be
defined.

From the set texts, give two examples of Attic literature.

"How to Convert a Loft" and "Insulation and You"

What aspects of a text would structuralist critics look at?

THE BUILDINGS

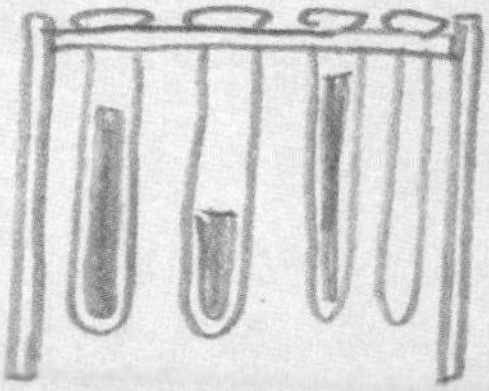

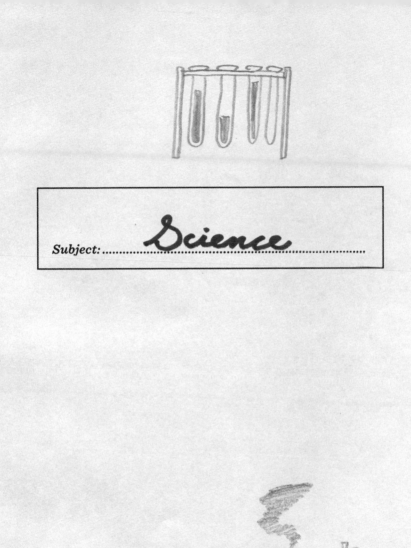

Subject: Science

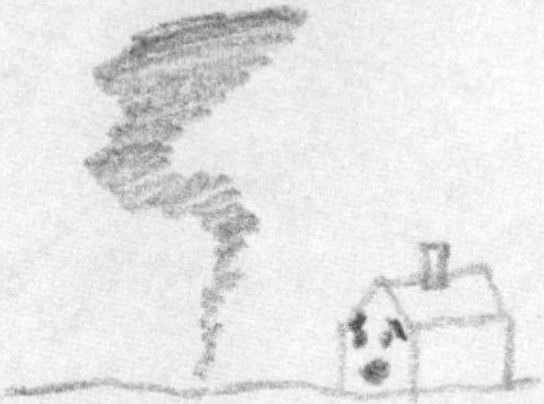

Why are white peppered moths likely to be more common than black ones in country areas?

RACISM

Why was Lamarck's theory of evolution discredited?

Because no one knew who he was.

Describe the properties of a meteor.

An animal that only eats meat

Explain the process of evolution.

SEVERAL MILLION YEARS

Describe energy produced by the human body.

Nervous energy

What is a genetically modified organism?

Something like a wig which has been made to make a bald person look like they have hair.

Describe a neutrino.

The opposite of an oldtrino.

There has been a marked rise in the percentage of carbon dioxide in the Earth's atmosphere over the last 50 years; suggest one reason for this.

Breathing. Breathing.
Breathing. Breathing. Breathing.
Breathing. Breathing.

Frog numbers are falling rapidly. Explain the effect this will have on the insect population.

They will have a party.

Describe the purpose of cytoplasm.

In Ghostbusters II it was used to make the Statue of Liberty come to life. I've never seen it used since.

What is the unit "Calorie" used to measure?

HOW MUCH SOMEBODY WILL
COMPLAIN ABOUT THEIR
WEIGHT.

In this food web, what is represented by arrows?

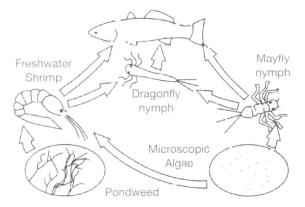

Freshwater Shrimp

Dragonfly nymph

Mayfly nymph

Microscopic Algae

Pondweed

WHO FANCIES WHO

What conclusions can be drawn about the universe from redshift?

It's becoming more
right-wing

Define a supersaturated solution.

Water with extra water in it.

What is the symbol for iron?

My Mum does this

What is an artificial pesticide?

Someone who is only
pretending to be really
annoying.

Explain the term "half-life."

When someone goes out
and has fun half the time.

What does a covalent bond involve?

A secret friendship between nuns.

Why are catalytic converters fitted to cars?

To make sure no cats get run over.

What is beta radiation?

Radiation that's nearly complete, but needs to be tested.

What is a step-up transformer?

It's the sequel to Step Up
and Transformers where
the humans teach the
robots to dance.

Earth is closer to the Sun than Mars, and bigger. What are two other differences between the two planets?

1. Color.
2. Aliens.

Explain the process of thermal energy transfer.

cuddles!

Explain the difference between potential energy and useful energy.

potential energy talks a lot but doesn't do much. useful energy is less fun but more helpful.

Give one advantage, in any research project, of having a large sample size rather than a small sample size.

You can see it better.

At the end of a marathon, a runner covers herself in a silvered space blanket. Explain how the space blanket keeps the runner warm.

Alien technology.

The diagram shows a van and a car. The two vehicles have the same mass and identical engines. Explain why the top speed of the car is greater than the top speed of the van.

Van   Car

It has go-faster stripes.

What is a pathogen?

Some one who
doesn't believe
in war.

A study found that the use of energy-saving light bulbs meant a boiler requires more gas to heat a house.

The most likely explanation for this is that . . .

They LIED

Bioethanol is a biofuel. What does this mean?

Here is your
answer!

Explain two of the benefits of hydroelectric power stations.

1) It keeps the Hydra busy so Hercules can do other things.

2) Hydra's heads grow back, so it's a renewable energy source.

Despite high fuel costs, it is still cheaper to generate electricity from fossil fuels or nuclear than it is from wind.

This is mainly because . . .

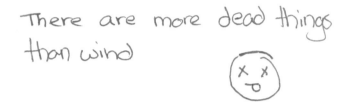

There are more dead things than wind

What is the advantage of nuclear fuels?

Accidents cause Superpowers.

Explain why the copper pipes inside a solar panel are painted black.

The engineers were big Rolling Stones fans.

It is important for our health to have a clean environment in our homes. Name two common pollutants in the home.

1. My brother
2. The dog

What are the key differences between aerobic and anaerobic respiration?

"an"

Give two similarities between an eye and a camera.

1) The Round bit.

2) They both blink.

Before taking blood, a nurse dabs some alcohol onto the patient's arm. This makes the patient's skin feel cold.

Explain what happens to make the patient's skin feel cold.

A nurse dabs some alcohol onto the patient's arm

Coronary heart disease is an illness affected by hereditary factors. Name two hereditary factors that affect your health.

Your mom's health and your dad's health.

Subject: *Psychology and Sociology*

What ethical issues might arise regarding an experiment involving children?

Children can't be trusted.

What would be one way of selecting a sample of schoolchildren? What would be the advantages and disadvantages?

Choosing the tallest ones. No disadvantages — they all have a better vantage point.

How would a child's education be affected by growing up in poverty?

They would learn how to bargain hunt.

Give one reason why someone would not want to vote in a general election.

They might only want to vote in a specific election

Outline the Oedipus Complex.

How can a study avoid being affected by individual difference?

Ask The same person
100 times

What benefits are there to using a closed-question survey rather than one with open questions?

Yes.

What is the disadvantage of using official statistics?

You can't make things up.

How reliable are methods for measuring stress?

Not very - if you're stressed you'll probably not take very accurate measurements.

In sociology, what does Action Theory state?

No matter how many bad guys are shooting at him, the hero _never dies._

Argue for one side of the nature vs. nurture debate.

I ARGUE FOR T̲H̲I̲S̲ SIDE

Discuss the changing nature of social class

it changes every year as we get older e.g. we'll be in 8th grade next year.

Give an example of a primary source. Explain why it is a primary source.

Tomato sarce because nearly everyone loves it

How does Neo-Marxism differ from Marxism?

Its followers all wear brightly colored clothes.

What assumption does the developmental
approach make?

THAT YOU WILL DEVELOP
MENTAL PROBLEMS
EVENTUALLY

What happens during the operationalization stage
of the research process?

The surgeons get
to work

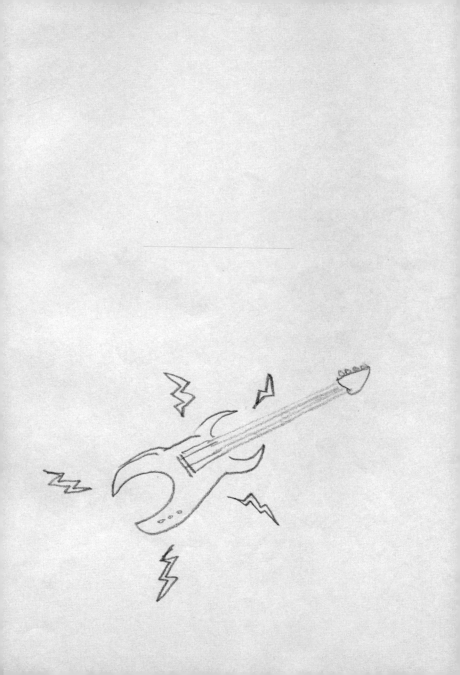

Subject: *Performing Arts*

What is meant by a cappella?

A smaller than normal hat.

What are the main features of baroque music?

It can't be fixed.

Give an example of a sonata. What makes your example a sonata?

FRANK SONATA. HE WAS BORN
A SONATA.

In music terms, what is a vamp?

Are you telling me
there's a Twilight
musical? OMG

What is the Italian term for a change of speed in music?

How does a mezzo soprano differ from a soprano?

What is the importance of the performer in modern theater?

It would be a really boring play without any actors.

What effect do the comic characters in Shakespeare's non-comic plays have?

They ruin the mood.

What elements of a play could be evaluated and developed as it is created?

The bad parts.

Discuss what is most important out of lighting, sound, and costume?

Costume, unless it is a nudist play

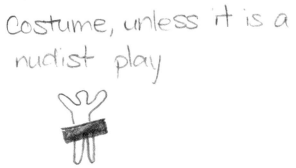

What is a monologue?

When one person won't shut up.

What are the key differences between a waltz and a march?

A waltz is a type of dance.

A march is what soldiers do.

When a score instructs you to play an arpeggio, what does this mean?

It's getting too big for its boots!.

Discuss the effect of theatre technology in one cotemporary piece.

ROBOTS ARENT VERY EMOTIVE

Give an example of an effective use of staging.

Successfully building a stage.

What elements should be included in a stage ground play?

a stage, the ground

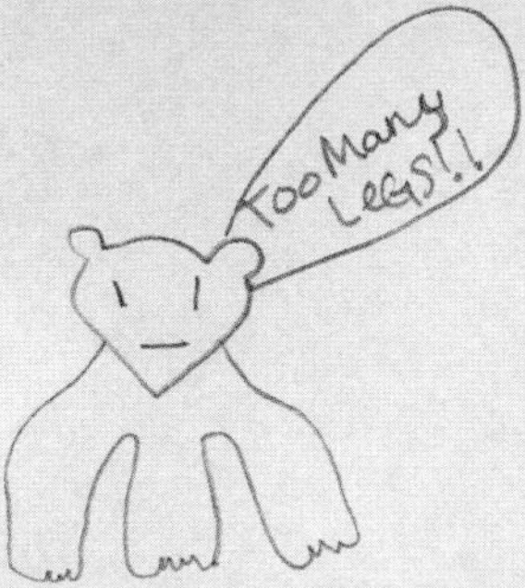

TooMany LeGS!!

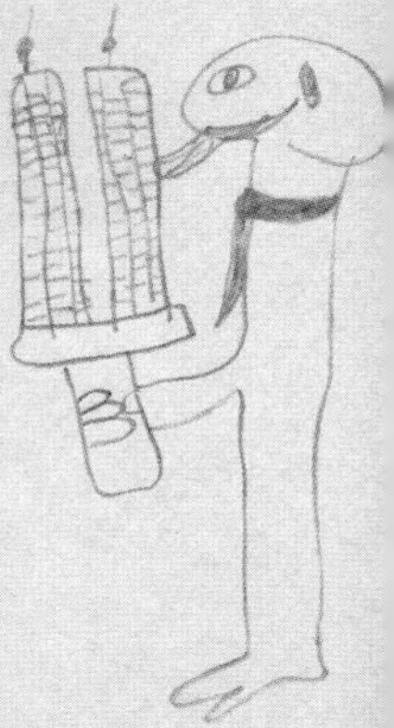

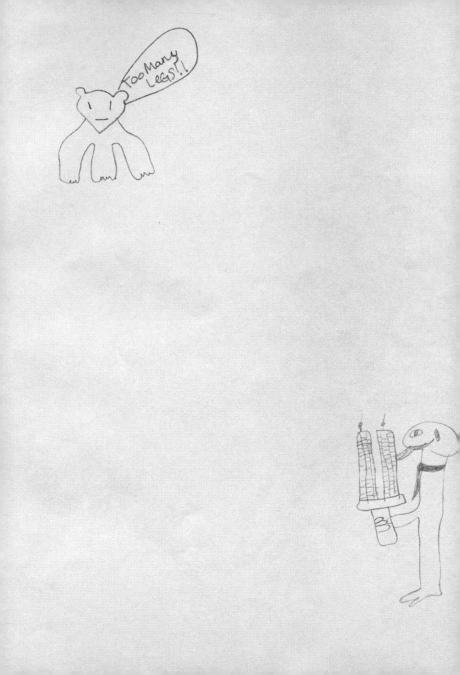

Subject: .... *History* ....

What is meant by a federal state?

a place where everyone
has to wear a hat

In politics, what does the term "impeachment" mean?

Its like imprisonment,
but with fruit

What changes would a codified UK constitution bring about?

More people eating cod.

Who sits in the Council of the European Union?

Saruman.

What was the armistice?

It's similar to legistice, but for arms.

What was the cause of the Hungarian Revolution in 1956?

They were getting hungarier and hungarier

What was the Truman Doctrine?

A more trustworthy version
of the Falseman Doctrine

What do the letters NATO stand for?

Not
At
The
Office

What problem rocked the USSR in 1986?

Provide a summary of the events of the Boston Tea Party.

Everyone had a cup of tea and some cake.

What were the terms of the Treaty of Versailles?

Autumn term, Spring term, Summer term

Why was the "Glorious" Revolution of 1688 called such?

Because it was just fabulous, darling!

Provide two names that Elizabeth I was known by.

"Your Majesty" and "Please Don.t Cut My Head Off."

For what reason was James I also known as James IV?

THEY COULDN'T COUNT.

How did King Cnut reprove his courtiers?

He cnutted them.

Name two attributed qualities of Richard the Lionheart.

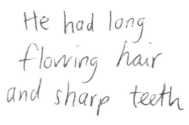 He had long flowing hair and sharp teeth

Why was James II known as the Great Pretender?

He was the most talented member of the Pretenders.

What happened to heavy industries during the Depression?

THEY GOT HEAVIER, AS PEOPLE EAT WHEN DEPRESSED.

What is another name for the "Roaring Twenties"?

The "Shouting Post-Teens"

What were the events leading up to the
St. Valentine's Day Massacre?

Someone didn't get
any cards.

Name the four humors of Greek medicine.

Slapstick, irony, wordplay, and poo jokes

What is meant by the term "prehistoric"?

BEFORE ANYONE CARED ENOUGH TO WRITE IT DOWN.

What is the Hippocratic Oath?

an oath you don't intend to keep.

Imsety, Hapy, and Duamutef are examples of what?

the seven dwarfs

What did an Ancient Egyptian embalmer do?

EMBALMED ANCIENT
EGYPTIANS.

Describe an Ionic column.

A column that's
deliberately contrary
to its expected meaning.

What contributed to the Bronze Age collapse?

RUST

What factors contributed to the fall of the British Empire?

everybody got bored of eating fish and chips all the time.

Give a brief description of the Malthusian Trap theory.

you put cheese in the trap.

What was Chamberlain's plan of appeasement?

That peas should be served alongside fish and chips.

What was the Poor Law Act of 1388?

it made it illegal to be poor.

What is the definition of an oligarchy?

A society where
ugly people
are in charge.

ME

cat rubber

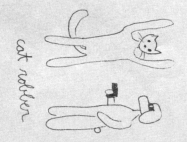

Math and Economics

Subject: ....

Calculate the mean of this group of numbers:

2, 12, 5, 8, 4, 18, 8

Eight looks quite mean

The diagram shows a fair spinner.

Which color is the arrow least likely to land on?

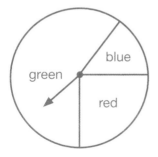

Yellow

If tickets to a football game cost $12.50 each, how much would it cost Johnny and his three brothers to go?

$12.50 each

Lisa wants to knit two types of sweaters, one requiring 2½ balls of wool and one requiring 1¾ balls, using only 4 balls of wool. Can she do it?

ONLY IF SHE CAN ACTUALLY KNIT.

Samuel gets $15 a week for doing his chores.
His parents increase this by $2 on his fourteenth
birthday. What does he get after this?

A gambling problem

James's monthly outgoing costs are $50 on his
mobile phone, $80 on utilities, $450 on rent, and
$80 on savings. Draw and label a pie chart to
represent his outgoing costs.

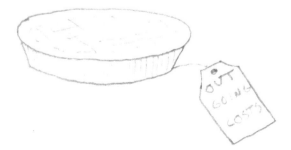

A train that normally travels at an average of 60 mph leaves 30 minutes late. If it increases its average speed to 65 mph will it be on time?

NO!! TRAINS ARE NEVER
ON TIME...

This pictogram shows the school lunches for the week.

Pasta	○ ○
Chilli	○ ◁
Fish	○ ◖
Curry	⌓
Soup	

Key: ○ = 4 lunches

How many times was curry eaten in the week?

Pac-Man!

Oscar has three orange cards and nine green cards. What is the probability he picks a blue card?

⁹⁄₁₂ IF HE'S COLOR BLIND.

A block of metal is 4 cm tall, 5 cm long, and 10 cm deep. What is the volume of the block?

Very quiet, unless dropped, then very loud.

Draw a tetrahedron.

Using supply and demand, explain the increase in the price of gasoline.

Gas station owners
Demand that drivers
Supply them with
more money

4 9 3 5

Use these digits to create:

The smallest four-digit number they can make:

4935

The largest four-digit number they can make:

Describe trends in passenger numbers using UK airports.

at the moment there are lots of florals and pastel colors.

In what ways are monopolies a negative thing for consumers?

It's really boring and takes about 8 hours to finish a game.

What is meant by the term "negative equity?"

A miserable horse

What advantages and disadvantages does the market domination of supermarkets have for consumers?

Advantage — all the markets are now SUPER

Complete the pie chart to show how a
government minister might organize spending.

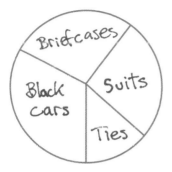

How could a country decrease the import of
foreign goods?

By not importing them

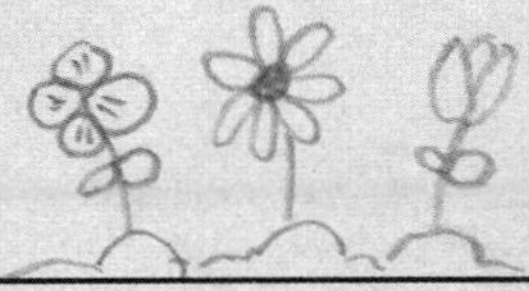

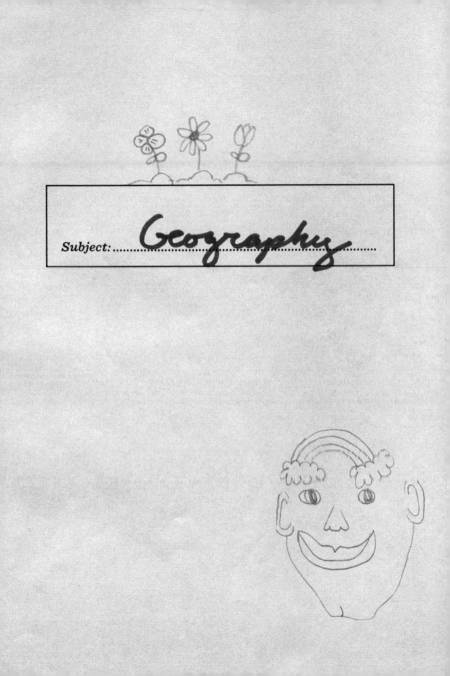

Subject: Geography

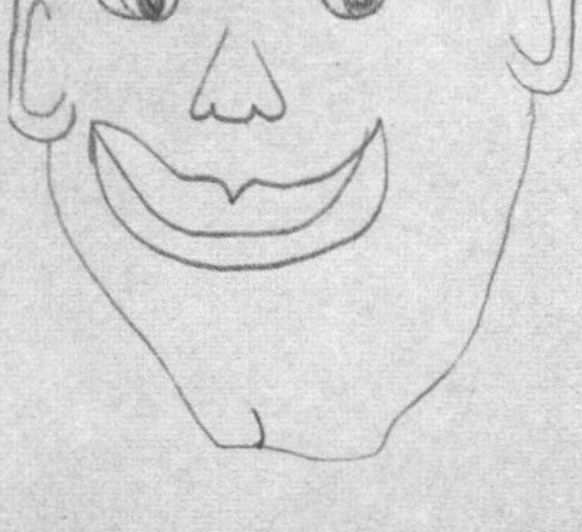

Where can you find the Andes?

Google Earth.

Why can flooding be beneficial?

IF YOU'RE ON FIRE.

What are plants that are able to store water called?

clever.

Name one cause of avalanches.

yodelling

How are sedimentary rocks formed?

That's sedimentary, my dear Watson.

How much of the world's water is stored in the seas and oceans?

A lot !!.

What is created when a river runs over alternating layers of hard and soft rock?

glam Rock.

What is the mouth of a river?

It is how the river eats.

How are waves created?

1. Lift your arm
2. Shake your hand back and forth

What is it called when areas of coastline are allowed to erode and then flood naturally?

Laziness

There are many different ways in which the sea erodes the coast. Explain two ways in which the sea erodes the coast.

1. Nibbling
2. Biting.

Some people agree with the building of coastal defenses while others disagree with it. Why is this?

Some people will disagree with anything.

How old is the Earth?

Years.

What do the geological time periods relate to?

We have geography at
11am on Wednesdays and
Fridays.

Give an example of a supervolcano.

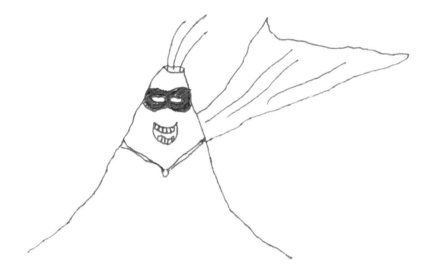

Where do hurricanes normally form?

IN THE AIR

What is meant by a "fragile environment"?

a glass house

What is the purpose of dams?

Similar to "blast"
and "gah!"

Which part of the Earth is directly below the crust?

the filling

Which part of the British Isles experiences the shortest days during the winter and the longest days during the summer?

France

What does the term "latitude" refer to?

It's French for attitude.

Describe two ways of reducing the demand
for water.

1. When it's yellow let it mellow
2. When it's brown flush it down

Name a factor that might attract a multinational
corporation to a country.

nice beaches.

What is it called when a foreign country invests in a country?

Investment

Name a negative impact of globalization.

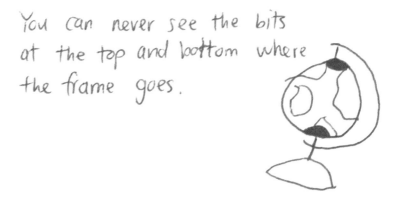

You can never see the bits at the top and bottom where the frame goes.

What is meant by population density?

How stupid people are.

Migration from a country may have both positive and negative effects. Describe these effects.

Positive: Moving somewhere nice!,

Negative: moving somewhere horrible!

Describe some ways that pollution problems could be reduced in cities in poorer parts of the world.

GET RID OF
THE COWS

What factors affect the sustainability of food sources?

How much people like
the taste of them

Explain the terms "subsistence farming" and "nomadic farming."

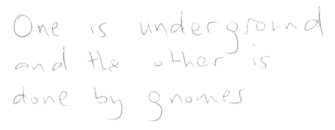

One is underground
and the other is
done by gnomes

Give one positive aspect of organic farming.

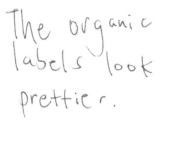

The organic
labels look
prettier.

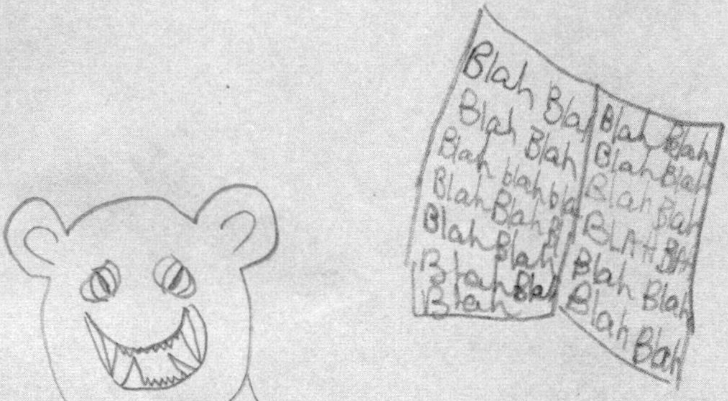
Blah
Blah Bla
Blah Blah
Blah blah bla
Blah Blah bl
Blah Blah
Blah Blah
Blah
Blah Blah
Blah Blah
Blah Blah
BLAH Bla
Blah Blah
Blah Blah

Subject: *Extra Credit*

I will...

Give two examples of computer input devices and what they are used for.

Left hand and right hand

How does ROM function differently than RAM?

It's less violent than RAM

What is OCR?

A sort of yellowish color

What sort of program would you use to do a mail merge?

I'd put something boring on so not to distract me from sorting all the envelopes

Who plans strategies for a team?

M̶r̶.̶ ̶I̶.̶
Hannibal

How can television provide a public service?

Showing fewer reality
shows.

How has the nature of magazine publication
changed in the past 30 years?

There is less nature
to publish photos of
because of global
warming!

How are television advertisements aimed at their
target audience?

through the screen

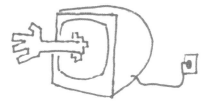

What will concessions mean for some groups at sports facilities?

ADMITTING
DEFEAT

What is the name of an unpaid participant in sports?

Slave.

Name ONE factor that will increase sports participation.

INCREASED SPORTS

What must sportspeople do before taking part in a sports activity?

get to where a
Sports activity
is taking place

FAILURE
is Always an Option

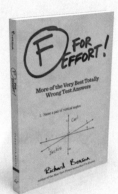

National Best Sellers!

Faced with a question they have no hope of getting right, these students decide to have a little fun instead.

$9.95 • PB

 CHRONICLE BOOKS